The Publishers gratefully acknowledge assistance provided by Dame Ursula Twebbin, M.Mmbop (Oxon), Grand Leopardess of the Imperial Order of Wifecraft, in compiling this book.

Publishers: Ladybird Books Ltd, Loughborough

Printed in England. If wet, Italy.

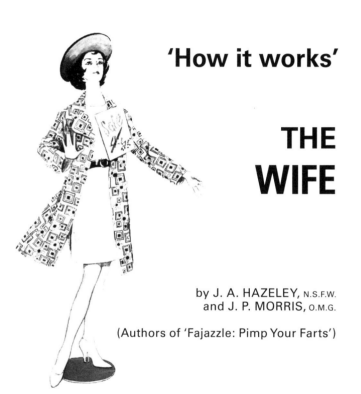

'How it works'

THE
WIFE

by J. A. HAZELEY, N.S.F.W.
and J. P. MORRIS, O.M.G.

(Authors of 'Fajazzle: Pimp Your Farts')

A LADYBIRD BOOK FOR GROWN-UPS

This is a wife.

She looks happy, doesn't she?

This is because she is on her second glass of wine.

Wives like to be right.

Sara has been waiting for her husband Tom to arrive. He is half an hour late.

Sara is delighted. She knew this would happen.

The wife is good at inventing things — new toys, new recipes, new outfits.

After a tiring day of inventing, the wife needs reviving with wine.

If she drinks enough wine, at the end of the week she invents a story for the recycling man about having had a big party.

Tina is getting married. It is the best day of her life.

Next year, she will claim that becoming a mother was the best day of her life, but only because she was on some very strong drugs.

Neither is true. The best day of her life was her eighth birthday, when she got a yellow bike.

Sasha likes baking because it is something for the children to do.

Sasha's children do not like fruit cake. Sasha's husband does not like fruit cake.

Luckily, it all gets eaten.

Wives and husbands both like gadgets.

Ian has bought Victoria a hoover, an iron, a sewing machine, a washing machine, a food mixer, a hairdryer, a kettle and a toaster.

He has also bought himself a record player, so he can stay out of Victoria's way while she enjoys her new gadgets.

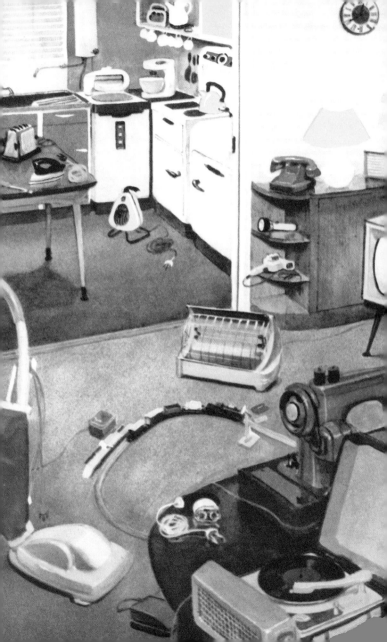

The wife likes to plan ahead. She measures out her life in meals.

Even at breakfast, she is only three mealtimes from her first glass of wine.

Samantha likes magazines that explain why other wives look disappointing on holiday.

She reads them on the train and throws them away before she gets to work.

Samantha does not want the other wives at work to judge her as one of those wives who enjoys judging other wives.

Laura's sister is getting married this weekend at an exciting faraway location, and everyone is invited.

Laura's family now cannot afford to go on holiday this year.

"This is worse than the hen do at the earth's core," thinks Laura.

When a wife feels sad, she eats chocolate.

Chocolate makes the wife happy.

But eating chocolate makes her worry about her weight and her skin, which makes her feel sad.

Still, there's always chocolate.

Today, Celeste is looking after her nephew and nieces. She is not used to children in the house, and they do ask a lot of questions.

She has had to open a bottle of emergency wine.

"Only another eight hours to go," thinks Celeste.

Science has concluded that the average wife needs more and more cosmetic and hygiene products every year to function normally.

Scientists like Christopher have discovered that the average husband requires no cosmetic products, because he is already so very beautiful.

Helen does not mind where she goes on holiday this year, as long as it is where she has been dropping hints she wants to go since last October. She thinks it is obvious. It is Kerala.

Stuart must work out the correct destination from Helen's clues. His best guess so far is something to do with rice.

He has checked his atlas, and there is no Rice Coast.

Maria thinks it is high time she and Mike faced up to a few things.

Mike thinks high time is some years away yet.

Rosie is a member of a fitness club.

There she has tried crossfit, spin and ultra-ballet.

Her £600 annual membership meant that each visit last year cost £200.

Emma eats salad, because it is not fattening.

This is also why she drinks wine instead of cream or gravy.

Six months after having her first baby, Rosie is going back to work.

Sadly, like half of all new parents, she is now worth less money to an employer.

Luckily, there are simple jobs Rosie can do.

Sometimes the wife needs a break.

Gail is happy she has managed to find a few hours with her best friends, away from her home, her husband and her children.

They are all relaxing by talking about their homes, their husbands and their children.

The wife likes surprises.

Her favourite sort is a surprise birthday party.

It is the husband's job to organise this surprise for her, and to keep her informed of every detail about it.

Wives like to talk.

Phil's wife Imogen had a furious go at him last night about how he avoids talking to her.

Phil feels bad about this today, and is making it up to Imogen by mending the roof.

After ten years of marriage, Kelly is trying some bedroom rôle-play with Ben.

Ben is pretending to be a brave fireman. Kelly is pretending to be a woman who has set fire to her house.

Sometimes marriage makes wives do things.

Karen and Amanda have come to a get-together in the same outfit.

They have each been discussing what they will wear today for five months. But at the last minute Karen has changed her mind.

Amanda says she won't let it spoil her wedding.

While her husband is away at a conference in Vancouver, Mel has indulged in a little on-line "retail therapy".

She has ordered two Scotsmen — a red one and a green one.

She will try both, and return the one she likes less.

Wendy has drawn these cards for her husband Daniel, so he has a handy pocket reference to how she feels.

She is going to test him later.

Wendy's ex-boyfriend won the Booker Prize last week.

This is Daniel's last chance.

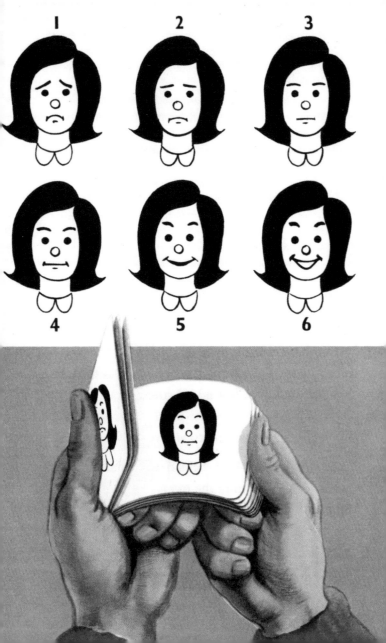

The authors would like to thank the illustrators whose work they have so mercilessly ribbed, and whose glorious craftsmanship was the set-dressing of their childhoods. The inspiration they sparked has never faded.

MICHAEL JOSEPH

UK | USA | Canada | Ireland | Australia
India | New Zealand | South Africa

Michael Joseph is part of the Penguin Random House group of companies whose addresses can be found at global.penguinrandomhouse.com

First published 2015
004

Printed in Italy by L.E.G.O. S.p.A

A CIP catalogue record for this book is available from the British Library

ISBN: 978–0–718–18354–7

www.greenpenguin.co.uk

MIX
Paper from
responsible sources
FSC® C018179

Penguin Random House is committed to a sustainable future for our business, our readers and our planet. This book is made from Forest Stewardship Council® certified paper.